THE 10

Greatest
Accidental Inventions

Jack Booth

Series Editor
Jeffrey D. Wilhelm

Much thought, debate, and research went into choosing and ranking the 10 items in each book in this series. We realize that everyone has his or her own opinion of what is most significant, revolutionary, amazing, deadly, and so on. As you read, you may agree with our choices, or you may be surprised — and that's the way it should be!

Franklin Watts®

an imprint of

SCHOLASTIC

www.scholastic.com/librarypublishing

A Rubicon book published in association with Scholastic Inc.

Ru'bĭcon © 2008 Rubicon Publishing Inc.
www.rubiconpublishing.com

 is a trademark of The 10 Books

Associate Publishers: Kim Koh, Miriam Bardswich
Project Editor: Amy Land
Editor: Christine Boocock
Creative Director: Jennifer Drew
Project Manager/Designer: Jeanette MacLean
Graphic Designer: Brandon Köpke

The publisher gratefully acknowledges the following for permission to reprint copyrighted material in this book.

Every reasonable effort has been made to trace the owners of copyrighted material and to make due acknowledgment. Any errors or omissions drawn to our attention will be gladly rectified in future editions.

"Baking the World's Biggest Cookie" (excerpt from "The Big Oven"). Provided by Immaculate Baking Co.

"Health worries repel Scotchgard" (excerpt) by Jim Quinn. © McClatchy Tribune Information Services. All Rights Reserved. Reprinted with permission.

"Stainless Steel." From WGBH Educational Foundation, Copyright © 2000 WGBH/Boston.

Cover: Glass and hammer–Getty Images/Photodisc/200247300-001

Library and Archives Canada Cataloguing in Publication

Booth, Jack, 1946–
    The 10 greatest accidental inventions / Jack Booth.

Includes index.
ISBN 978-1-55448-510-9

    1. Readers (Elementary). 2. Readers—Inventions.
I. Title. II. Title: Ten greatest accidental inventions.

PE1117.B6612246 2007a   428.6   C2007-906706-9

1 2 3 4 5 6 7 8 9 10   10   17 16 15 14 13 12 11 10 09 08

Printed in Singapore

Contents

6

18

38

SERENDIPITY
— A LUCKY HAPPENING

Do you think inventions come about after years of hard work by scientists in laboratories? Many inventions do. But the truth is, a lot of important things that we use today were invented by accident, or serendipity. Someone made a mistake — and it led to the creation of something fabulous. Or, someone stumbled upon something, made a brilliant connection, and the result? Eureka! As simple as that! Serendipity!

The 10 things in this book fit our criteria of what makes an amazing accidental invention. Think about these criteria as you read. These inventions changed our lives and the world around us. They improved our way of life. They helped cure diseases and made it possible for us to live longer and healthier lives. They had an impact on industry and business. And they are widely used and have endured for years.

As you read about these lucky accidents, ask yourself:

Eureka: *Greek for "I have found it"; exclamation to celebrate a discovery*

WHAT IS THE GREATEST ACCIDENTAL INVENTION?

Gooey chocolate chip cookies taking shape in the oven

CHIP COOKIES

ESSENTIALS: Originally called Toll House Chocolate Crunch Cookies, today we know them as chocolate chip cookies.

TRIED-AND-TRUE: According to a *Bakery Production and Marketing* newsletter, 52 % of Americans choose chocolate chip as their favorite cookie.

NOTABLE NUMBERS: The Hershey Company estimates that seven billion chocolate chip cookies are eaten every year!

How can a cookie make it onto a list of the world's greatest accidental inventions? Well, just think about it. You've probably eaten dozens, if not hundreds, of chocolate chip cookies in your lifetime. And so have most of your friends. Some stats say that half of all cookies eaten in North American homes are chocolate chip! And, it's all thanks to a small substitution made years ago by an adventurous baker.

Today, chocolate chip cookies are part of mainstream American life. "[They] rank alongside apple pie and fried chicken as the most timeless ... of American foods," says writer Jonathan Levitt. When we think of national icons, we usually think of historic sites or important people. It's rare for a cookie to make this list. But, just as maple syrup is a symbol of Canada, chocolate chip cookies and America go hand in hand!

Chocolate chip cookies have sweetened our lives for over 70 years. For a mistake, that's incredible staying power!

CHOCOLATE CHIP COOKIES

Ruth Graves Wakefield

ACCIDENTAL GENIUS

Ruth Graves Wakefield is remembered as the unintentional inventor of the celebrated chocolate chip cookie. Wakefield worked as a dietician and lecturer. In 1930, she and her husband opened the Toll House Inn in Whitman, Massachusetts. The building was originally a toll house, where travelers paid a toll to rest, feed, and water their horses. The famous cookie was born in the inn's kitchen.

dietician: *someone who studies nutrition and eating habits*

A magnified cocoa bean

Quick Fact

Mayans first made chocolate drinks from cocoa beans around the 7th century A.D. They even used cocoa beans as currency!

MOMENT OF TRUTH

One fateful day in 1937, Wakefield was making her popular chocolate butter drop cookies. Normally, she mixed baker's chocolate, which melts completely, into the dough. That day, Wakefield used semi-sweet chocolate. She chopped it up and mixed it into the dough. Instead of melting, the pieces stayed intact. A new cookie was born!

END RESULT

Customers loved Wakefield's invention! The recipe was published in newspapers around New England. Wakefield had used a chocolate bar given to her by Andrew Nestlé (sound familiar?), who had visited the inn. After Wakefield's invention, sales of the delicious Nestlé Semi-Sweet Chocolate Bar skyrocketed. Wakefield's recipe was printed on every wrapper. In 1939, Nestlé first introduced chocolate chips.

Quick Fact

Chocolate chips contain less cocoa butter than regular chocolate. Cocoa butter is the natural fat of the cocoa bean. It makes chocolate smooth. Because they have less cocoa butter, chocolate chips hold their shape when heated.

? Think of other foods that have become identified with America. What do you think it takes for a food item to achieve this status?

BAKING THE WORLD'S BIGGEST COOKIE!

In 2003, North Carolina's Immaculate Baking Company baked the world's largest chocolate chip cookie. It weighed more than 40,000 pounds, the weight of four elephants! It was 102 feet in diameter — that's more than the length of a basketball court! This account, from Immaculate Baking Company, takes us behind the scenes to show us exactly how this huge treat was baked.

The BIG oven

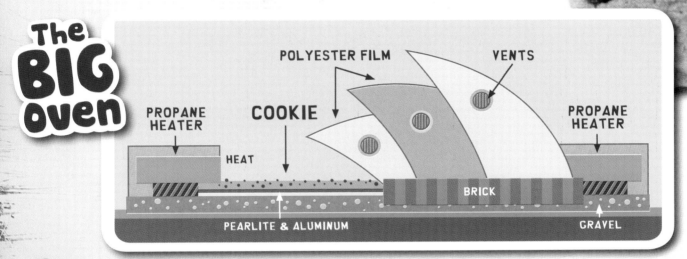

POLYESTER FILM VENTS

PROPANE HEATER COOKIE PROPANE HEATER

HEAT

BRICK

PEARLITE & ALUMINUM GRAVEL

One of the first questions we're asked about the World's Biggest Cookie is "How'd you bake THAT?" Well, it wasn't easy! From the day we set our goal for 100 feet, we began tossing ideas around. The Guinness rules made it a true challenge: The cookie had to be baked all at once instead of baked in sections and pieced together. ... It wasn't long before we sought expert consultation. ... [T]hese guys quickly created a design for a structureless oven made from materials you could purchase at your local hardware store! The concept was very simple ... [W]e would create a layered base made with gravel, pearlite (the white stuff in potting soil), and aluminum sheets on top to serve as a pan. This combination shielded the cookie from the cool ground temperatures of May. We would then cover the oven with layers of polyester film (the material helium balloons are made of) to keep the heat trapped inside. Finally, we surrounded the pan with over 20 heaters which, together, were capable of raising the oven temperature to well over 350°F!

---

potting soil: *enriched soil used for plants in pots*

The Expert Says...

"Today the chocolate chip cookie remains a favorite choice among cookie connoisseurs."

— Linda Stradley, author, culinary historian, and creator of the "What's Cooking America" Web site

Take Note

Chocolate chip cookies have endured for 70 years and are an American icon. But, they haven't had much impact on our lives except to make us smile, so they crunch in at #10.
- Canada's obsession with Tim Hortons donuts has earned it the label "Timbit Nation." A Timbit is a donut hole from the Tim Hortons chain of restaurants. Think of an original slogan that captures the way Americans feel about chocolate chip cookies.

5 4 3 2 1

Only one company, Velcro International, is legally allowed to use the name "Velcro." All other companies producing similar products must use terms like "hook and loop," "burr," or "touch" fasteners.

You might not recognize the name George de Mestral, but you definitely know about one of his inventions. You probably use it almost every single day.

George de Mestral is the inventor of Velcro, a hook and loop fastener that handily holds things together and is easy to close and pull apart. Today, it is used everywhere, from clothing to construction, and even in space travel!

When you get dressed in the morning, you might use Velcro tabs to fasten your jeans and jacket instead of zippers and buttons. Or maybe you use Velcro tabs to fasten your running shoes (it beats tripping on an untied shoelace!). The next time you secure your backpack or pockets with Velcro patches, just think of George de Mestral — the person who made it all possible.

And it all came about because he took his dog for a walk in the fields around his home. Talk about serendipity!

VELCRO

ACCIDENTAL GENIUS

George de Mestral was born in Lausanne, Switzerland, in 1907. He lived in this area his whole life. From an early age, de Mestral had an inventive mind and was fascinated by engineering and science. At the age of 12, he designed a new kind of model plane and received his first patent for it. De Mestral graduated from the Federal Institute of Technology in Lausanne, Switzerland, as an electrical engineer.

Quick Fact

People tend to use the name Velcro for all hook and loop fasteners, even ones made by other companies. The same has happened with Q-tips, tupperware, and champagne!

MOMENT OF TRUTH

Returning from a walk through the fields with his dog one day, de Mestral discovered that his clothes and his dog's fur were covered in burrs. It took forever to pull them off. De Mestral was intrigued. He put some burrs under his microscope and discovered that each one was like a ball with thin strands sticking out. Each strand had a hook, or barb, at the end. With his engineer's mind, de Mestral applied nature's idea to create a very useful item.

patent: *document giving an inventor total control over his or her invention*

burrs: *rough or prickly coverings of a plant*

Quick Fact

The National Inventors Hall of Fame in Akron, Ohio, honors inventors who have successfully patented their amazing inventions. George de Mestral was inducted into the Hall of Fame in 1999.

END RESULT

It took years of experimenting for de Mestral to make his product perfect. Finally, he found that nylon sewn under infrared light formed the toughest hooks. De Mestral's invention was incredible because it was strong yet easy to pull apart. In 1955, de Mestral finally got a patent for his hook and loop creation. De Mestral formed Velcro Industries to manufacture his invention. People loved the new product because it was easy to use and very effective. He was soon selling more than 60 million yards of his invention per year!

infrared light: *electromagnetic radiation with wavelengths longer than visible light but shorter than radio waves*

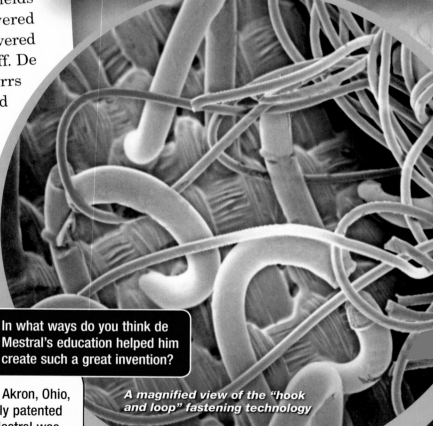

? In what ways do you think de Mestral's education helped him create such a great invention?

A magnified view of the "hook and loop" fastening technology

From Sneakers to Spacesuits!

Hook and loop fasteners can be found in some pretty unusual places. Read this list to discover some surprising uses for this accidental invention.

- To avoid things floating away in zero gravity, NASA has used hook and loop fasteners for years to hold toothbrushes and other items to spacecraft walls!

- NASA also uses this type of fastener to attach equipment and tools to astronauts' suits. To help astronauts avoid dehydration on spacewalks, small bags holding water are attached to the insides of their helmets with Velcro.

- To Velcro Wall Jump, participants wear a suit made of the hook side of the fastener. They then catapult themselves onto a loop-covered wall. Just don't ask how they get down once they're stuck!

dehydration: *excessive loss of water from the body*

Astronaut James S. Voss (left) and cosmonaut Yury V. Usachev in front of the Payload Equipment Restraint System (PERS), which uses Velcro to restrain equipment in zero-gravity situations.

The Expert Says...

" Where does invention come from? One of the most powerful ideas is … to see something that nature has invented and use that as an inspiration. … There is one terrific example: Velcro. "

— Nathan P. Myhrvold, founder and CEO of Intellectual Ventures, an invention company

Take Note

Velcro clings to the #9 spot. While chocolate chip cookies merely sweeten our lives, Velcro has made life much easier in many ways and has several handy uses.

- List the ways you use Velcro in your daily life — without repeating the uses already mentioned in this piece.

5   4   3   2   1

This invention is made up of different chemicals. The particles in the substance are sticky on one side, so they attach to fabrics, and slippery on the other, allowing stains to slide right off.

ESSENTIALS: Scotchgard is a stain and dirt repellent that was first sold in 1956.

TRIED-AND-TRUE: 3M, the company that manufactures Scotchgard, sells hundreds of millions of dollars worth of it every year.

NOTABLE NUMBERS: There are more than 10 products based on Scotchgard now sold by 3M.

The truth is that people spill stuff. It happens all the time. Carpets and couches are constantly in danger from sticky soft drinks and gooey foods! Spills don't look too pretty, but thanks to chemical researcher Patsy Sherman and her assistant Samuel Smith, they aren't the disasters they used to be.

Today, all-purpose Scotchgard protector is used on everything from clothes and carpets to eyeglasses and sofas. It's so effective that we almost take spills for granted! And, we owe this peace of mind to a fortunate accident. Sherman and Smith weren't trying to invent a fabric protector when they happened upon the magic formula. But, they stumbled upon a mixture of chemicals and synthetic latex, or plastic, that repelled oil and water from fabrics. They were smart enough to realize how many uses this invention could have!

Sherman and Smith's find didn't really change the world. But, it has kept it cleaner! For helping to keep so many things from getting wrecked, Scotchgard earns the #8 spot on our list.

---

synthetic latex: *artificial rubber*

SCOTCHGARD

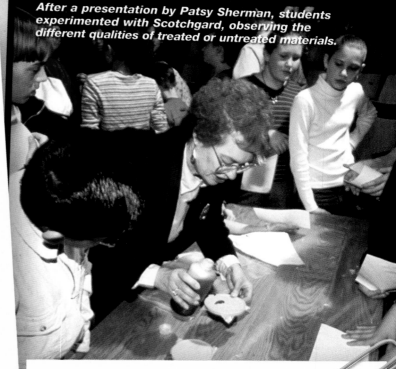

After a presentation by Patsy Sherman, students experimented with Scotchgard, observing the different qualities of treated or untreated materials.

ACCIDENTAL GENIUS

Sherman was born in Minneapolis, Minnesota, in 1930. In 1952, she graduated from college with degrees in chemistry and mathematics. Smith was born in New York City and attended the University of Michigan. Sherman became a research chemist at 3M in 1952, a year after Smith joined the company. In 1953, the scientific duo was working on a project at the 3M laboratories in St. Paul, Minnesota. They were trying to create a new type of rubber to be used in airplane fuel lines.

MOMENT OF TRUTH

One day, Sherman handed a bottle containing a synthetic latex mixture to her assistant. Smith dropped the bottle. Some of the liquid splashed onto Sherman's white shoes. The two tried to clean it off with soap and other cleaners, but these just beaded up. The coating on the shoe was repelling other substances.

research chemist: *scientist who studies and experiments with chemicals*
repelling: *resisting; not sticking to or mixing with*

END RESULT

The duo immediately recognized the potential uses for their discovery! Using their chemical know-how, they created a winning product. They created a substance that didn't alter the feel of fabrics, but did repel stains and spills. In 1956, 3M introduced Scotchgard.

Quick Fact

Sherman once said, "[Anyone] can become an inventor as long as they keep an open and inquiring mind and never overlook the possible significance of an accident or apparent failure."

apparent: *appearing as such but not necessarily so*

The Expert Says...

"Crucial to Scotchgard's success was the ability... to see the product potential when that chemical was spilled ... Without such perceptiveness, there would be no Scotchgard.

— Bob Gatty, Washington-based writer, editor, and publisher

perceptiveness: *understanding; insight*

8

7

6

In 2003, 3M released reformulated and environmentally friendly versions of its famous Scotchgard products. This newspaper article will help you understand why.

Health Worries Repel Scotchgard

Milwaukee Journal Sentinel, by Jim Quinn
July 30, 2000

The world just got a little harder to clean.

Because of potential environmental and health concerns, the 3M Co. announced ... it would stop producing a product that has made life a little easier for almost 50 years. Scotchgard has been the most important stain-repellent ... since 3M started selling it in 1956.

... Things went fine for Scotchgard until the 1990s. ... [This was] when environmental scientists developed new, more sensitive instruments for measuring [pollution] ... Tests revealed that Scotchgard molecules had spread more widely through the environment than ever suspected.

The company found the chemical in the bodies of most Americans. Chances are, your blood contains Scotchgard.

"It's in a lot of different locations," said Bill Coyne, senior vice president of research and development at 3M. Coyne said there's no evidence that these tiny traces do any harm.

The problem, he said, is the widespread nature of the contamination.

molecules: *small particles; tiny bits*
contamination: *pollution*

? Scientists sometimes don't know how their inventions might affect the environment. What are some other fabulous inventions that have had unexpected negative effects?

Take Note

A failed lab experiment and a dirty pair of tennis shoes might have spelled a bad day for Patsy Sherman. But, thanks to her background in chemical engineering, she knew that the synthetic latex stuck to her sneaker had potential! Today Scotchgard is used everywhere and on everything. It has helped us to keep our homes, clothes, and cars clean. Velcro is convenient, but Scotchgard's spotless reputation ranks #8.

• Sherman was a research chemist at 3M. What kinds of projects do you think research chemists work on? What kinds of companies do you think they work for and why?

When it first came out, the microwave was considered a space-age cooking wonder. According to advertisers, this 1960s version could "crisp bacon in 90 seconds!"

OVEN

ESSENTIALS: Microwave ovens cook by causing the molecules inside food to move very quickly. This friction creates heat and cooks food!

TRIED-AND-TRUE: The microwave oven is the first truly new way to heat food since people learned to cook with fire thousands of years ago.

NOTABLE NUMBERS: The first microwave ovens stood over 6 ft. tall and weighed more than 770 lb.!

Today, millions of homes around the world have one. Just think about how many times each day you use a microwave oven. Your morning routine might involve zapping some instant oatmeal. Maybe you like to munch on microwaved popcorn while watching TV. Thanks to microwave ovens, we can quickly and efficiently defrost, reheat, and cook food.

Believe it or not, this modern-day convenience started out as a wartime invention. During World War II, a piece of equipment called a magnetron was invented. A magnetron is a key part of a radar machine. Radar works by bouncing electromagnetic waves off objects. During the war, radar machines were used to detect the location of enemy planes, warships, and submarines.

So how does this relate to the microwave oven sitting on your kitchen counter? One day in 1946, an American scientist named Percy Spencer was working with a magnetron in a lab. When a candy bar in his pocket melted, Spencer had a mess to clean up, but he also had an idea. What if magnetrons could be used to cook food? Spencer followed his instinct. He went on to invent a machine that changed the kitchens of millions of people!

electromagnetic waves: *forms of energy emitted as radio waves, X-rays, and so on*

MICROWAVE OVEN

Percy Spencer

ACCIDENTAL GENIUS

Spencer was born in Howland, Maine, in 1894. He never finished high school, but in 1912 he joined the Navy to become a radio operator. He had a lot of catching up to do! "I just got hold of a lot of textbooks and taught myself while … standing watch at night," Spencer once said.

? "The educated scientist knows many things won't work. Percy doesn't know what can't be done." What do you think a co-worker meant when he said this about Spencer?

Quick Fact
The waves used in microwave ovens are radio waves. Apart from cooking, radio waves are used to transmit radio frequencies, to carry TV and phone signals, and in many other ways.

MOMENT OF TRUTH

Spencer had a reputation for being curious and determined. But fate, or hunger at least, had to step in before he made his life-changing discovery. In 1946, Spencer was working at Raytheon, a company that made and supplied equipment to the military. Spencer noticed the melted candy bar while he was working on simplifying the process of making magnetrons. He realized that a magnetron's waves, or microwaves, had melted the candy. Spencer also realized that he had stumbled upon something revolutionary. Microwaves weren't just for radios and radar machines, they could also be used to cook or melt all kinds of foods!

END RESULT

Spencer started experimenting right away. He set popcorn kernels in front of the magnetron tube, and he soon had freshly-popped popcorn. Spencer discovered that the magnetron's electromagnetic waves made water, sugar, and fat molecules in food vibrate more quickly. This caused friction. All that movement created heat and cooked whatever the waves had passed through. In 1945, Raytheon patented the first microwave oven.

Quick Fact
The first commercial microwave oven was available in stores in 1947. It was called the Radarange. It wasn't until 1967 that smaller, cheaper microwave ovens became popular household items.

The Expert Says…

"When it was first introduced, the microwave oven was considered a gimmick. Today, it's as essential as the kitchen sink."

— Ann Steiner, co-author of *Microwave Know How*

WHAT'S REALLY GOING ON?

You don't need to be a molecular scientist to know how a microwave works. Just check out this labeled diagram and explanation.

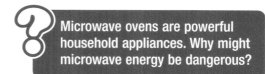
Microwave ovens are powerful household appliances. Why might microwave energy be dangerous?

STIRRER

WAVE GUIDE

MAGNETRON

METAL MESH

POP!

FILTER

TRANSFORMER

MICROWAVES CAUSE MOLECULES TO VIBRATE AND FOOD TO COOK

A microwave oven is basically a strong metal box. The front door is usually made of plastic or glass, which is protected with a layer of metal mesh that prevents microwaves from escaping.

Each microwave oven contains an electronic tube called a magnetron. When you press the on-button, the magnetron takes electricity from the outlet. This is converted into a type of radio wave. These microwaves are blasted into the metal box through a wave guide. Inside, the microwaves are bounced off the microwave oven's metal walls. The microwaves are absorbed by the food. They excite the water and fat molecules, which causes the food to heat up. Plastic, glass, and paper do not absorb any microwaves, so the waves pass right through these materials without heating them up.

excite: *stimulate; agitate*

Quick Fact

In 2007, scientists at the University of Florida discovered an easy way to sterilize nasty household sponges. Microwaving wet sponges on full power for only two minutes killed 99% of bacteria and viruses!

Take Note

The microwave oven revolutionized the way people cook. It made life speedier and more convenient. We love Scotchgard for the protective barrier it provides between us and spills. But for getting dinner on the table in minutes, the microwave oven comes in at #7.
• People love microwave ovens because they're so fast. But we still use regular ovens and other cooking appliances. Why do you think this is?

5   4   3   2   1

Vulcanized rubber, such as the rubber used in these tires, was named after Vulcan, the Roman god of fire. Today, tires are one of the world's biggest uses for vulcanized rubber.

RUBBER

ESSENTIALS: In 1770, scientist Joseph Priestley found that the dried sap from some tropical trees could rub out pencil marks; he called the substance *rubber*.

TRIED-AND-TRUE: Charles Goodyear first patented vulcanized, or weatherproof, rubber in 1844.

NOTABLE NUMBERS: The Goodyear Tire & Rubber Company was founded in 1898, nearly 40 years after Charles Goodyear's death.

The story of vulcanized rubber goes back to the days of explorer Christopher Columbus. In 1493, Columbus returned to the islands he called the West Indies. Here, he saw people playing with balls made of the hardened sap of native trees. Columbus and his men thought the new material, which would later be called rubber, was a miraculous discovery.

Columbus took some of the material back to Europe. He hoped that it would be extremely useful. But, he soon realized rubber wasn't the miracle product he thought it was! It had a strong odor. In hot weather, it melted into a gooey mess. In cold weather, it turned brittle and shattered like glass. For hundreds of years rubber had very limited uses.

Then, in 1839, Charles Goodyear stumbled upon a way to improve rubber. Vulcanization prevented rubber from hardening. Vulcanized rubber was permanently elastic. It didn't melt in heat or crack in the cold. Soon, people were wondering how they had ever lived without it! It's not just rubber, it's vulcanized rubber, and it takes the #6 spot on this list.

---

vulcanization: *treatment to make rubber stronger and more elastic*

VULCANIZED RUBBER

ACCIDENTAL GENIUS

Charles Goodyear was born in New Haven, Connecticut, in 1800. He worked at his family's hardware business but became an inventor when he was 33. In 1834, Goodyear tried to sell a valve he had invented for rubber preservers to the Roxbury India Rubber Company. They weren't interested. Their business was in trouble because rubber wasn't selling well.

MOMENT OF TRUTH

After becoming an inventor, Goodyear became obsessed with trying to create weatherproof rubber. He tried mixing rubber with different chemicals and powders. He heated it and cooled it, but the rubber was still affected by extreme temperatures. Goodyear was unsuccessful until one day in 1839 when he accidentally dropped a glob of a rubber-sulphur mixture onto a hot stove. As he scraped up the charred rubber, he knew he had stumbled upon something great!

END RESULT

The new material was firm and flexible. After being out in the cold for hours, it was still bendable! The vulcanized rubber wasn't sticky, didn't smell, and didn't rot. Goodyear spent five years perfecting his invention. He eventually discovered the perfect amount of sulphur and heat needed to make rubber completely weatherproof. In 1844, Goodyear patented his vulcanized rubber.

? It took Goodyear more than five years to invent vulcanized rubber. But he never gave up. What does this tell you about this inventor? What can you learn from someone like Charles Goodyear?

Charles Goodyear trying to perfect his rubber formula

Quick Fact

Amazingly enough, Charles Goodyear had no direct connection to today's Goodyear Tire and Rubber Company. Founder Frank Seiberling merely named the company in honor of Goodyear.

Quick Fact

Too much of a good thing? According to the Goodyear Company, after perfecting weatherproof rubber, Goodyear dressed in rubber hats, ties, and shoes. Among other things, he wanted to make rubber money, jewelry, and flags!

8   7   6

RUBBERIZED WORLD

Latex sap from a rubber tree is collected in a cup

This **chart** will teach you more about latex's journey from nature to industrialization.

A synthetic racing tire

From Nature

- Rubber trees have soft tissue under their bark. This is where liquid latex is found. People tap the trees to extract the latex sap, which is made into rubber.

- Natural rubber comes from trees growing in rainforests and tropical places. Pará rubber trees, or *Hevea brasiliensis*, are used for most commercial production. This is because when pará rubber trees are cut, they produce lots of sap to cover the wound.

- Dozens of trees, shrubs, and plants, including dandelions, lettuce, and milkweed, contain latex. But, since these plants are relatively small, it's not cost effective to use them for making rubber.

- We use latex to make rubber. For plants, sticky, toxic latex is a good defense against insects that might eat them!

Modernized!

- The late 1800s saw a huge demand for vulcanized rubber because of the invention of bicycles and automobiles. It also had many uses in machinery and industry, making it influential in the industrial revolution.

- In 1845, Stephen Perry of London, England, patented the first rubber band made from vulcanized rubber.

- Today, there are two kinds of rubber — natural and synthetic. Synthetic rubber is made from materials including petroleum, coal, oil, and natural gas.

- The first synthetic rubber was created around 1927, in Germany. By 1960, more synthetic than natural rubber was being used. This is still true today.

 This invention had a huge impact on transportation. Which other industries or areas of life have been improved by the inventions you have read about so far?

The Expert Says...

"Vulcanization made possible the many applications we think of today when we speak of the modern rubber industry. Tires, hoses, seals … etc., are but a few of the applications … that consume the approximately 40,000,000,000 pounds of rubber produced each year."

— Dr. Richard Farris, Distinguished University Professor Emeritus, Polymer Science and Engineering Department, University of Massachusetts Amherst

Take Note

Rubber wasn't very useful before Goodyear. His chance discovery allowed us to use this natural substance in revolutionary ways. Microwave ovens are great when you're in a rush to eat. However, vulcanized rubber has affected more areas of life so it ranks higher at #6.

- Do you think rubber should be made naturally, from trees, or synthetically, from fossil fuels? Which do you think is better for the environment, and why?

5   4   3   2   1

A shattered windshield — still in one piece thanks to the miracle of safety glass

SS

ESSENTIALS: Safety glass doesn't splinter into dangerous little pieces when struck or smashed.

TRIED-AND-TRUE: Since 1937, all cars have been required to have windshields made out of safety glass.

NOTABLE NUMBERS: Safety glass was first used in gas masks during World War I. It first appeared in windshields in 1924.

In the early 1900s, automobiles had only been around for a few years. Most people still preferred to use their horses to get around. Cars were expensive. But there were other reasons that people weren't rushing to buy these new inventions. At that time, cars had windshields made of ordinary glass. These were extremely dangerous, even in minor accidents. These windshields could easily shatter and send sharp pieces of glass flying into the air. When the first cars with glass windows on all four sides were introduced, people were afraid to ride in them!

Luckily, things would soon change. One clumsy French scientist, a crowded laboratory, and a fallen beaker led to the invention of safety glass. The rest, as they say, is history. With this invention, cars became much safer. So did public buildings, goggles, and many other items involving glass. People around the world are much safer thanks to this remarkable glass.

SAFETY GLASS

ACCIDENTAL GENIUS

Edouard Benedictus was born in 1878 in France. Not much is known about his childhood, but he did study to become a chemist. As a scientist, Benedictus was well-equipped to realize his lab accident was more than just a clumsy mistake!

> Benedictus had a very important impact on the safety of the world. But we know little about him. Why do you think this inventor is less well known than some others on our list?

MOMENT OF TRUTH

One day in 1903, Benedictus was busy working in his lab. Reaching for something, he accidentally knocked a glass bottle off a shelf. When he looked down, he was amazed to see that the bottle hadn't shattered. He had heard it crash but, instead of breaking into pieces, the glass had held together.

END RESULT

Benedictus discovered that the fallen beaker had recently contained cellulose nitrate, a liquid plastic. A thin layer of the plastic had coated the inside of the bottle. Benedictus was inspired. He knew his invention could be used to protect people from flying glass in car accidents. He started experimenting with coated glass. By 1914, safety glass was in production!

> Benedictus first patented safety glass in 1910. This invention made cars much safer, but it wasn't required on all vehicles until 1937. Why do you think car manufacturers might not have wanted to use it right away?

Quick Fact

Benedictus started experimenting the same day he broke the beaker. But it took him seven years to perfect his formula for safety glass.

Crash test dummy hits windshield

The Expert Says...

" [Think] about it: After brakes and seat belts, what's more important to the safety and comfort of a car's occupants than glass? "

— Scott Memmer, writer for automotive Web site Edmunds.com

10   9   8   7

Safety Glass Is Everywhere!

Every time you ride in a car, walk into a public building, or close a glass shower door, you are protected by either laminated or tempered safety glass. The following lists show common uses of each type of safety glass.

Quick Fact

Laminated glass has a layer of flexible plastic sandwiched between two layers of glass. This holds it together when shattered. Tempered safety glass is treated to be stronger than regular, un-tempered glass and to break into small, smooth pieces.

Laminated

- thermometers
- shower stalls
- greenhouse windows
- shopping mall doors and windows
- home and apartment windows
- airplane windows
- car windshields

? What reasons can you think of for the different uses of each kind of safety glass?

Tempered

- side and rear windows of cars and trucks
- computer monitors
- TV screens
- skylights
- refrigerator shelves
- oven doors
- microwave doors

Quick Fact

Safety experts disagree about whether side and rear car windows should also be made of laminated glass. If they were laminated, they would stop people from being ejected from the rear and sides. Unfortunately, this might also stop people from being rescued from a burning or submerged vehicle.

Take Note

All buildings, cars, and kitchens have safety glass in them. Vulcanized rubber had a big impact on many areas of life, from travel to athletics to manufacturing. But safety glass is significant for its role in making the world safer. It gets a higher ranking, at #5.
- Since they were first invented, cars have had some major overhauls to make them safer. What other improvements, apart from safety glass, have made cars a safer mode of transportation?

5   4   3   2   1

These shiny new rolls of stainless steel could become anything from appliances or cutlery to car parts or artificial hips!

ESSENTIALS: Stainless steel is lightweight and extremely strong. It doesn't stain, rust, or crumble.

TRIED-AND-TRUE: It is used to make everything from home appliances and pipes to vats used to store hazardous chemicals.

NOTABLE NUMBERS: Stainless steel is 100% recyclable and most new pieces of stainless steel contain at least 60% recycled material.

In 1912, the world was first introduced to stainless steel. But the story behind this invention goes back a lot farther. Stainless steel was really more than 3,000 years in the making! Around 1200 B.C., people first discovered how to make iron. Iron is the main component of stainless steel.

Iron helped people make strong tools, wheels, and other useful things. Steel was first developed around 300 B.C. — it was even stronger than iron. But steel rusted. It constantly needed to be cleaned or replaced. Just imagine eating your spaghetti with a rusty fork made of ordinary steel!

Luckily, a type of steel that could resist stains and rust was discovered in the early 1900s. And it was all thanks to an accidental observation! Since then, we've been using this invention in countless ways. Stainless steel has allowed us to construct huge bridges and buildings. Companies that build cars, ships, trains, and planes rely on this material. It has a vital role in small things, too. We make essential medical and dental equipment using stainless steel. It easily resists the heat and chemicals used for sterilization.

For being so useful in such important ways, stainless steel takes our #4 spot.

component: *element or ingredient*
sterilization: *destruction of bacteria that can cause infection*

Vulcanization made rubber more useful. Similarly, stainless steel was an improvement of a product that already existed. What other inventions have made something ordinary, extraordinary?

STAINLESS STEEL

ACCIDENTAL GENIUS

Harry Brearley was born in 1871 in Sheffield, England. His father worked in a steel factory and introduced him to steelmaking at a young age. When Harry was 12 years old, he went to work at the steel factory. By the time he was 20, he was an apprentice in the factory's laboratory.

MOMENT OF TRUTH

At the time of his discovery, Brearley was working at the Brown-Firth Research Laboratories in Sheffield. He was trying to make a new type of steel for gun barrels. He mixed basic steel with small percentages of other metals to make new alloys. Many of these experiments were unsuccessful and Brearley threw them away. One metal he mixed with the steel was chromium. This is a hard metal that resists rust. One day, Brearley noticed that the discarded sample of this mixture hadn't rusted like the others.

alloys: *substances consisting of mixtures of different metals, or mixtures of metals and non-metals*

END RESULT

The chromium and steel sample became the basis for stainless steel! It only took two months for Brearley to perfect the formula. But the beginning of World War I, in 1914, put a temporary stop to most stainless steel production. It wasn't until the 1920s that steelmakers were able to roll out stainless steel for all kinds of applications.

Quick Fact

Medical marvel! Apart from the more common uses, stainless steel is also used in the making of artificial hips and knees and the rods that secure broken bones in place.

Quick Fact

At first, the company Brearley worked for didn't think his discovery was that great. So he had a cutlery maker create some knives out of his new metal. People soon saw how well the knives resisted rust and damage!

? Stainless steel sounds pretty amazing, right? So, why do you think that the company Brearley worked for had to be convinced that it was such a great invention?

Harry Brearley

10

A Stainless Reputation!

American Experience, PBS

Explore one of the world's most useful inventions in this article about stainless steel.

The development of alloy steels introduced a variety of new metals ... [But] it was a certain combination of chromium and carbon that led to the discovery of the industry's most superior grade of steel — stainless.

... Harry Brearley, a British expert in the analysis of steel, was the first to realize [stainless steel's] practical uses ... Brearley quickly realized the benefits of a high-strength, rustless metal ... [He] introduced it to the cutlery industry in Sheffield, England. It became the first to mass-produce a stainless steel product.

Quick Fact

Stainless steel is the generic term for different grades, or kinds, of steel that have a minimum of 10.5% chromium. They all resist rust, corrosion, and tarnish.

Stainless steel, with its sleek, shiny surface and tremendous strength, is a marvel of technology. It has revolutionized most modern industries ... The non-corrosive and rust-resistant properties of stainless steel have made it essential in the preparation, delivery, and storage of food. Stainless steel is a standard in modern restaurant kitchens since it can be easily cleaned and dried ... [Stainless steel is lightweight and durable] ... [This] allowed the development of streamlining in transportation. The streamlined design of new trains, planes, and automobiles allowed for less wind resistance ... Stainless steel paved the way for modern technology ... [It] continues to influence our lives every day.

streamlined: *smooth shape designed to give less air resistance*

The Expert Says...

"There is hardly a material thinkable that has found its way to so many applications in such a short period of time as stainless steel."

— Sjef Roymans, Editor in Chief,
Stainless Steel World magazine

Think of things in your home that are made of stainless steel. Describe a problem that might arise with each item if it was made of another material.

Take Note

Without stainless steel, our world would look pretty different! Stainless steel led to the invention of countless other items. It also improved everything from the medical field to the construction industry. The story behind this invention and its amazing impact on all aspects of our lives lead to its rank at #4.

• Why is the idea of streamlining so important? In what ways has streamlining improved transportation and made it easier for people to get to where they're going?

4

5   3   2   1

3 DYNAMITE

Having a blast! Luckily this is a controlled explosion, but shouldn't he be wearing ear protection?

ESSENTIALS: Dynamite is a controllable chemical explosive.

TRIED-AND-TRUE: Alfred Nobel first patented dynamite in 1867. He eventually had dynamite factories in more than 20 countries.

NOTABLE NUMBERS: Dynamite made the biggest bang, but Nobel had patented 355 inventions by the time of his death in 1896.

Alfred Nobel's father was an engineer, an architect, and an inventor. So it was no surprise when Alfred Nobel followed him down the scientific path!

When he was 13 years old, Nobel was inspired by the discovery of a powerful liquid explosive called nitroglycerine. It is more powerful than other explosives. At the time, people thought it was too dangerous. They thought it was too hard to control to be useful. But Nobel had other ideas. He wanted to find a way to control the size and timing of nitroglycerine explosions.

Nobel experimented for years, but nothing worked. It took a slippery test tube, a box of sawdust, and sharp powers of observation for Nobel to find success! "Safety Blasting Powder," what we now call dynamite, was the product of a lab accident.

Dynamite is a powerful tool. Its use led to great changes around the world. It allowed us to build roads and railways through mountains and across rough terrain. It was essential in the creation of the Hoover Dam and Mount Rushmore. Also, the Panama Canal, a vital shipping lane connecting the Atlantic and Pacific Oceans, couldn't have been built without dynamite. For its explosive impact, dynamite ranks #3.

DYNAMITE

ACCIDENTAL GENIUS

Nobel was born in 1833 in Stockholm, Sweden. In 1842, the Nobel family moved to St. Petersburg, Russia. Nobel traveled to Paris and studied to become a chemical engineer. In 1860, he put his education to use experimenting with nitroglycerine. Three years later, Nobel moved back to Sweden. He set up nitroglycerine factories there and continued experimenting.

END RESULT

Thanks to his slippery fingers, Nobel figured out that when mixed with sawdust, nitroglycerine became stable. He discovered that when he mixed a fine sand called *kieselguhr* (kee-zuhl-goor) with nitroglycerine, it made a paste. Nobel was then able to form the paste into rods or tubes. These tubes could be safely handled and exploded on demand.

Quick Fact

Close to nine million pounds of dynamite were used in the construction of the Hoover Dam. The dynamite was used to blast eight miles of tunnels through canyon walls!

Quick Fact

Nobel named his invention dynamite from the Greek word *dynamis*. This means power or powerful.

MOMENT OF TRUTH

One day in the lab, Nobel was holding a full test tube of nitroglycerine. The test tube slipped from his hand. To his surprise, the nitroglycerine didn't explode. Because the test tube had landed in a box of sawdust, the liquid had leaked out but there hadn't been an explosion. Nobel got an idea!

Alfred Nobel

Nobel once said, "If I have a thousand ideas a year, and only one turns out to be good, I'm satisfied." What does this say about Nobel's character? Does this mean he wasn't aiming high enough? Or, does this mean he was realistic? Explain your answer.

10   9   8   6

NOBEL'S LEGACY

There's a lot more to Nobel than dynamite. This anecdote about his legacy will blow your mind!

In 1888, one of Nobel's younger brothers, Ludvig, died. A French newspaper published an obituary of Alfred by mistake. The article called him "The Merchant of Death." The paper stressed the fact that Nobel had invented a product that was used to make bombs. Nobel was accused of causing many deaths with his invention. Nobel didn't want to be remembered this way. So, he decided to donate his wealth toward improving the world.

Alfred Nobel died in Paris, France, in 1896. He left orders in his will about how his fortune was to be used. He specified that cash prizes were to be given out every year in his name. These would be given for achievements in physics, chemistry, medicine, literature, and peace. Albert Einstein won the Nobel Prize in physics in 1921.

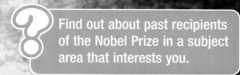
Find out about past recipients of the Nobel Prize in a subject area that interests you.

A Nobel Prize is one of the world's highest achievements. The awards are given out every year on December 10 — the day of Alfred Nobel's death. Nobel was able to change the way the world would remember him. Today, he is remembered for his practical inventions. But he is also recognized for his legacy to the world.

obituary: *notice of death that includes a description of the person's life*

The Expert Says...

" Dynamite was the first truly safe and predictable explosive ... It was one of the most significant technical developments in a century known for revolutionary inventions. "

— Stephen R. Bown,
historical nonfiction author

Take Note

Without dynamite, many of the world's greatest structures could not have been built. Stainless steel also helped in construction, but for helping us to navigate our world, dynamite ranks #3.
• Why might some people think dynamite isn't such a great invention? What are the unavoidable downsides to dynamite?

5   4   **3**   2   1

② X-RAYS

People absorb some of the radiation from every X-ray, and too much radiation can be harmful. Lead vests and other safety measures help protect us when we have an X-ray.

ESSENTIALS: X-rays are a type of electromagnetic radiation, just like visible light and microwaves.

TRIED-AND-TRUE: X-rays are vital because they can reveal broken bones and other serious health problems.

NOTABLE NUMBERS: According to market research company Theta Reports, an estimated 1.7 billion medical and dental X-ray procedures are performed around the world every year!

So what's so special about X-rays? They're just a kind of photograph, right? Wrong. Photographs are a record of what was in front of the camera when the camera's button was pressed. X-rays, on the other hand, go deeper. They show what's under the surface. They can pass through almost any kind of material — paper, glass, certain metals, even human flesh — to take pictures of what lies beneath!

If you've ever been to a dentist's or doctor's office, you've probably seen an X-ray machine. Doctors use X-ray machines to examine broken bones, find swallowed objects, and track growing tumors. Dentists use X-rays to find cavities buried deep inside your teeth. And this invention has important uses outside of the hospital and the dentist's office. X-rays at the airport are used to inspect baggage for weapons. They are used in manufacturing to inspect products. They have even been used by NASA to find flaws in the metalwork of space shuttles.

The impact X-rays have had on the world is impressive considering their accidental beginnings in 1895. The man who invented them, Wilhelm Röntgen, was the first scientist to receive a Nobel Prize in Physics for his work. This important invention ranks #2 on our list.

X-RAYS

ACCIDENTAL GENIUS

Röntgen was born on March 27, 1845, in Germany. In 1869, he graduated with a doctorate from the University of Zurich, Switzerland. Röntgen went on to become a university professor and the head of the physics department at several different universities. It was in 1895, at the University of Würzburg, Germany, that Röntgen made his discovery. He was researching cathode rays, which are beams of electrons used today in televisions and computers.

doctorate: *one of the highest academic degrees given by a college; degree of a doctor*

Quick Fact

"X" is the mathematical symbol for an unknown. Röntgen called his discovery X-rays because he wasn't quite sure what was causing them. The name stuck, and we're still calling them X-rays today!

Röntgen experimenting with cathode rays in the dark

MOMENT OF TRUTH

Röntgen was working in a darkened lab. He wanted to know if he could see cathode rays in the dark. He was experimenting with passing cathode rays from a generator through a vacuum tube. Röntgen wrapped the vacuum tube in dark paper. When he turned on the power, he noticed a weird, green light coming from across the dark room. It was coming from a piece of cardboard covered with a fluorescent mineral called barium platinocyanide (plat-eno-sigh-an-ide) Röntgen had accidentally left it lying on a bench. Röntgen knew cathode rays couldn't travel that far.

END RESULT

Röntgen knew that the tube was giving off a different kind of radiation or ray. These new rays could travel distances and pass through various materials. They could make the screen across the room glow! Röntgen started experimenting. One day, he held a small piece of lead in the path of the ray. Röntgen got a big surprise! The screen showed an outline of the bones in his hand. What a discovery!

generator: *machine that converts one form of energy into another*
fluorescent: *bright and glowing as a result of absorbing radiation*

Quick Fact

Röntgen's wife was the first person ever officially x-rayed. She held her hand between the cathode ray tube and a photographic plate. Röntgen took this picture showing the bones in her hand and her wedding ring!

10   9   8   7   6

A Clearer Picture

This article about X-rays will get you ready for your next checkup!

X-rays are a kind of "invisible light" that can pass through solid objects. Have you ever seen film negatives from a camera? X-ray pictures look like these. Hard material, like bone, appears white. Softer materials, like muscle, appear gray or black. These are harder to see on an X-ray. Because of this, doctors often need a little help when trying to get a closer look at an organ or muscle. For a clearer view, doctors have patients drink a substance called a *contrast medium*.

A contrast medium is a liquid that absorbs either a greater or a lesser number of X-rays than soft tissue. Positive contrast media strongly absorb X-rays. Negative contrast media don't absorb them at all. So, when a doctor wants to see how a patient's digestive tract is working, the patient swallows a liquid positive contrast medium. This mixture highlights the digestive tract. The X-ray will show exactly where the contrast medium has gone down! This allows the doctor to spot any problems.

Negative contrast media, like oxygen or carbon dioxide, are also sometimes used. These don't absorb X-rays, so instead of highlighting areas, they make them look dark.

 Calcium is one of Earth's most abundant minerals. Bones and teeth are full of calcium. Why do you think X-rays can't pass through calcium? If you don't know, find out.

The Expert Says...

"Today, [Röntgen's] mysterious rays are used to diagnose and treat a wide range of medical problems … The X-ray has paved the path for safer and more sophisticated technologies, such as the ultrasound and MRI."

— Rhonda Rowland, former CNN medical correspondent

A radiologist examines an X-ray of an intestine highlighted by a positive contrast medium.

X-rays let us see inside our bodies to examine potential problems. If we didn't have X-rays, how would we know what was wrong? What other methods might help doctors diagnose patients?

Take Note

X-rays make it easier for doctors to diagnose patients. They also make airports safer and are used in manufacturing to inspect products. Dynamite allowed us to build in more places than we had ever thought possible. But for their role in health care and security, X-rays rank #2.
• A radiologist is a type of doctor who is specially trained to read X-rays. Why is training to interpret X-ray images important?

5   4   3   **2**   1

A lot of the penicillin used today for medical purposes is synthetic, or artificial. Scientists made the first synthetic penicillin in 1946.

ESSENTIALS: Penicillin is made of the *Penicillium notatum* mold and can be used to fight infections and diseases.

TRIED-AND-TRUE: In 1941, a man dying from a *Staphylococcus* (staf-uh-loh-caw-kus) bacteria infection became the first person ever treated with penicillin.

NOTABLE NUMBERS: On D-Day, in 1944, penicillin was used to save thousands of wounded soldiers.

Putting antibiotic ointment on a cut might seem like a small thing. But this simple action can save your life! We take it for granted these days, but having the ability to kill harmful bacteria has given us all a new lease on life.

Not long ago, a tiny cut or scratch could kill a person! An open wound could easily get infected. This often led to amputation, or worse. Bacterial infections could also make people very sick. It was common for children to die from throat infections. Strep throat wasn't as curable as it is today.

A discovery made in 1928 changed all this. A young scientist found a nasty growth in an unwashed petri dish. Luckily, he didn't throw it out and wash up. Instead, Dr. Alexander Fleming examined the mold. He noticed that it could kill harmful bacteria. What Fleming found led to his invention of penicillin. Dangerous bacteria are no match for this medicine! It has had an incredible impact on global health care. This life-saving drug easily earns the #1 spot on our list.

---

antibiotic: *substance that kills or disables bacteria and other tiny organisms*

PENICILLIN

ACCIDENTAL GENIUS

Fleming was born in Scotland in 1881. He became a doctor and a bacteriologist. Fleming was a captain in the Army Medical Corps in World War I. His battlefield experiences taught him how serious bacterial infections could be. After the war, Fleming went to work at St. Mary's Hospital in London, England. He was trying to find a cure for infections.

bacteriologist: *scientist who studies bacteria*

Penicillin is an important, life-saving medicine. But it can be very dangerous for people with penicillin allergies. Why do you think something that kills germs might also cause allergic reactions?

Quick Fact

Penicillin kills bacteria by destroying cell walls that the bacteria need to survive. These cell walls eventually burst, killing the bacteria.

MOMENT OF TRUTH

One day in 1928, Fleming was rushing around before leaving on vacation. He forgot to put some petri dishes into the incubator. When he returned, he found mold growing on a dish of *Staphylococcus* bacteria. Different species of these bacteria cause food poisoning, skin infections, and diseases. *Penicillium notatum* mold thrives in cool temperatures. It wouldn't have grown if Fleming had put his dish in the incubator before leaving!

Quick Fact

Antibiotics are the most commonly prescribed medications in modern medicine. Overuse of antibiotics has made many bacteria resistant to them. As doctors prescribe higher doses, bacteria have gotten stronger and harder to kill.

END RESULT

Fleming discovered that bacteria near the mold were dying. Because it was a *Penicillium* mold, Fleming called the active ingredient penicillin. It took more than 10 years to figure out how to manufacture penicillin for widespread use. Two other scientists, Ernst Chain and Howard Florey, found out how it could be done.

incubator: *piece of equipment used to control environmental conditions*

Close-up of Penicillium notatum spores

Dr. Alexander Fleming at work in the lab

MIGHTY MOLD!

Read this timeline and find out how this mold rose to the top!

1928 — Alexander Fleming first discovers *Penicillium notatum*'s bacteria-fighting powers!

1929 — Fleming writes about his incredible find in a leading medical journal. But, since penicillin is so hard to grow and to use effectively, the medical community is slow to take notice.

1939 — A team of scientists, led by Howard Florey and Ernst Chain, begin to study antibacterial agents found in bacteria and molds.

1940 — Scientists Florey and Chain test penicillin on mice. They inject eight mice with deadly bacteria but only treat four with penicillin. The next day, the four mice given penicillin are still alive, but the other four have died.

1941 — Florey and a group of scientists travel to the U.S. to test new sources for mold production. The group discovers that cantaloupe melons produce a particularly productive strain of *Penicillium notatum* mold.

1941 — Penicillin is used for the first time on a patient. A man dying from a *Staphylococcus* bacteria infection is treated with penicillin. Since penicillin is still only available in small quantities, there isn't enough to treat him with and he dies.

1943 — Penicillin is mass-produced for the first time.

> **?** In 1945, Fleming, Chain, and Florey all received the Nobel Prize for Medicine. Do you agree that each of them deserved to receive the prize? Why or why not?

The Expert Says...

" By the middle of the century, Fleming's discovery had spawned a huge pharmaceutical industry, churning out synthetic penicillins that would conquer some of mankind's most ancient scourges. "

— Dr. David Ho, Director of the Aaron Diamond AIDS Research Center

scourges: *causes of great suffering or trouble*

Take Note

The X-ray is our #2 greatest accidental invention because it allows doctors to look inside our bodies and treat us. But penicillin takes the #1 spot. It has protected us from diseases and infections that were once life-threatening. It has also helped us live longer, healthier lives.

• Penicillin comes from a naturally occurring mold. But today, a lot of penicillin is synthetic. Why was it important for scientists to be able to make synthetic penicillin?

5 4 3 2 1

We Thought …

Here are the criteria we used in ranking the 10 greatest accidental inventions.

The invention:
- Had a lasting impact
- Improved health care
- Led to modernization
- Inspired other great inventions
- Is used all over the world
- Has made the world a safer place
- Made life more convenient

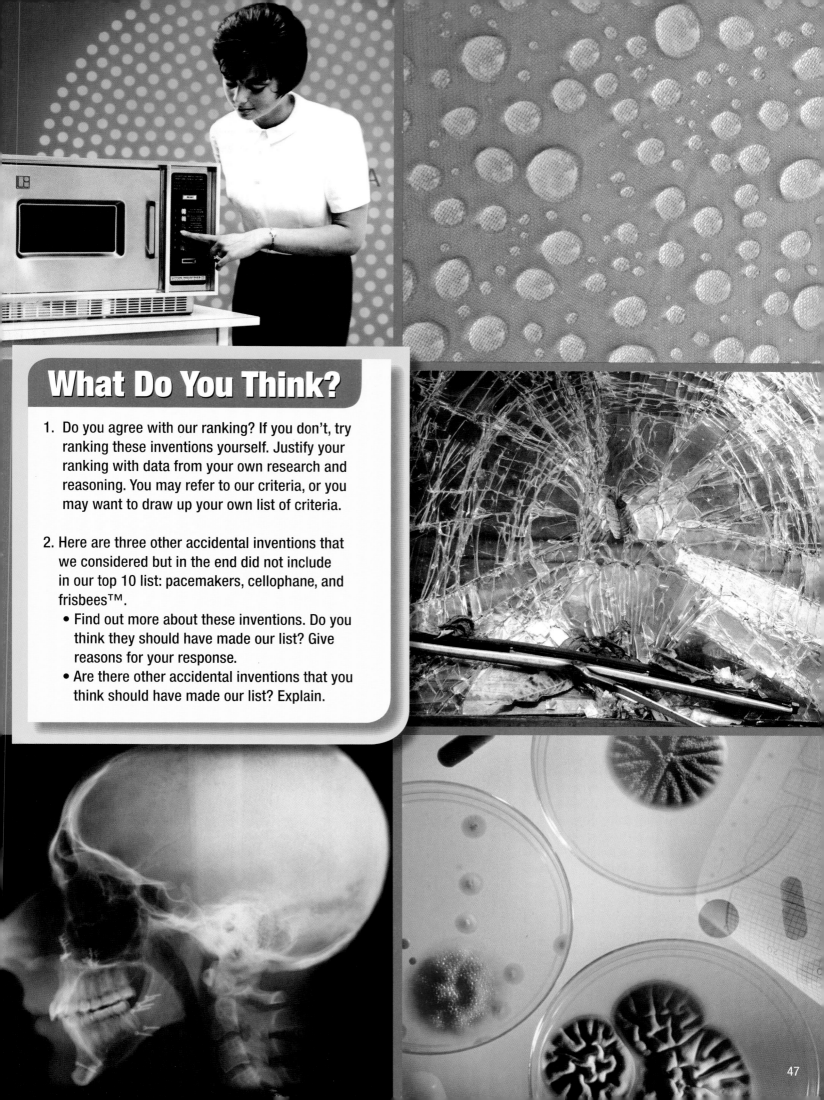

What Do You Think?

1. Do you agree with our ranking? If you don't, try ranking these inventions yourself. Justify your ranking with data from your own research and reasoning. You may refer to our criteria, or you may want to draw up your own list of criteria.

2. Here are three other accidental inventions that we considered but in the end did not include in our top 10 list: pacemakers, cellophane, and frisbees™.

    *   Find out more about these inventions. Do you think they should have made our list? Give reasons for your response.
    *   Are there other accidental inventions that you think should have made our list? Explain.

Index